The [illegible] of John

William MacDonald

Emmaus Correspondence School
LUKE 24:27

Original text material by William MacDonald
Developed as a correspondence course by
Emmaus Correspondence School,
founded in 1942.

Unless otherwise noted all Bible quotations in this course are from the New King James version of the Bible. © 1982 by Thomas Nelson, Inc. Used by permission.

Published by:
ECS Ministries
P.O. Box 1028
Dubuque, IA 52004-1028
www.ecsministries.org

ISBN 0-940293-05-6

010203/06050403 (AK–03)

Printed in United States of America

Instructions to Students

The letters of John are practical. They can be disturbing too for John allows no shades of gray in our lives. With him things are either black or white, right or wrong, true or false, good or bad. God is light, and in Him is no darkness at all.

Thus these letters are especially relevant to our day and age. We are living in days when, so far as the world is concerned, the prevailing philosophy is that morals are relative and religion should be synthesized. John's writings blow such fuzzy cobwebs right out of the minds of God's people.

This study will challenge you to face squarely the absolutes of the Christian faith.

How This Course Is Organized

1. The Christian Fellowship (1 John 1:1–2:2)
2. Tests for Fellowship (1 John 2:3–28)
3. More Tests for Fellowship (1 John 2:29–3:24)
4. Still More Tests for Fellowship (1 John 3:24–4:21)
5. Further Tests for Fellowship (1 John 5:1–21)
6. John's Last Two Letters (2 John; 3 John)

How to Study

Begin by asking God to open your heart to receive the truths He would teach you from His word. Read the chapter through at least twice, once to get the general idea of its contents and then again, slowly, looking up all Scripture references and examining all footnotes. Remember, you may use a dictionary for any terms you do not understand.

Exams

The exams can be found in the center section of this course. Each exam covers one chapter (Exam 1, for example, covers chapter 1).

The Exam Booklet can be removed from the course book and, once the exams are completed, returned for grading. More information can be found in its Exam Booklet.

Study Schedule

Begin studying immediately, or if you are in a group, as soon as the group begins. We suggest that you try to complete one chapter each week and take a maximum of one year to finish the course.

How Your Papers Are Graded

Any incorrectly answered questions will be marked by your instructor. You will be referred back to the place in the Bible or the textbook where the correct answer is to be found. You will receive a certificate showing your grade.

Group Enrollments

If you are enrolled in a class, submit your exam papers to the leader or secretary of the class who will send them for the entire group to the Correspondence School.

Returning Your Exam

See the Exam Booklet for instructions on sending your exam for grading.

CHAPTER

1

The Christian Fellowship (1 John 1:1–2:2)

Introduction to First John

John's First Letter is like a family photograph album. It describes those who are members of the family of God. Just as children resemble their parents, so God's children have His likeness too. This letter describes the similarities. When a person becomes a child of God, he receives the life of God—eternal life. All who have this life show it in very definite ways. For instance, they acknowledge Jesus Christ as their Lord and Savior, they love God, they love the children of God, they obey His commandments and they do not go on sinning. These, then, are some of the tests of eternal life. John wrote this letter so that all who have these family traits may know that they have eternal life (1 John 5:13).

At the time John was writing, a false sect had arisen known as Gnostics. These people claimed to be Christians, but they said that they had additional knowledge, superior to what the apostles taught. Among other things, they taught that Jesus was just a man, born of Joseph and Mary. They said that the Christ was not a person but a mere influence that came out from God. According to them, Jesus was not Christ; rather the Christ came upon Jesus at the time of His baptism and left Him before He died on the Cross. John realized that these people were not real Christians, and so he warned his readers against them by showing that these Gnostics did not have the marks of true children of God.

According to John, a person either is a child of God or he is not; there is no in-between ground. That is why this letter is filled with such extreme opposites as light and darkness, love and hatred, truth and lie, death and life, God and the devil. At the same time, it should be noted that the apostle likes to describe people by their habitual behavior. In discerning between Christians and non-Christians, for instance, he does not base his conclusion on a single act of sin, but rather on what usually characterizes the person. Even a broken clock tells the correct time twice in every twenty-four hours. But a good clock tells the correct time regularly. So the general, day-by-day behavior of a Christian is holy and righteous, and by this he is known as a child of God.

John uses the word "know" a great many times. The Gnostics professed to *know* the truth, but John here sets forth the true facts of the Christian faith, which can be *known* with certainty. He describes God as light (1:5); love (4:8, 16); truth (5:6); and life (5:20). This does not mean that God is not a Person, but rather that God is the source of these four blessings. John also speaks of God as righteous (2:29; 3:7); pure (3:3); and sinless (3:5). While John uses simple words, the thoughts he expresses are often very difficult to understand. As you study these lessons, therefore, you should pray that the Lord will help you to grasp the meaning of His Word and to obey the truth as He reveals it to you.

The Person of Christ (1:1, 2)

The doctrinal foundation of all true fellowship is the Person of the Lord Jesus Christ. There can be no true fellowship with those who hold false views concerning Him. The first two verses teach His eternity and the reality of His incarnation. The same One who existed from all eternity with God the Father came down into this world as a real Man. The reality of His incarnation is indicated by the fact that the apostles heard Him, saw Him with their eyes, gazed upon Him with deep meditation, and actually handled Him. The Word of Life was not a mere passing illusion, but was a real Person in a body of flesh.

Verse two confirms that the One who was with the Father, and whom John calls "that eternal life," became flesh and dwelt among us and was seen by the apostles.

The Testimony of the Apostles (1:3, 4)

The apostles did not keep this wonderful news as a secret, and neither should we. They realized that the basis of all fellowship is found here and so they declared it freely and fully. All who receive the testimony of the apostles have fellowship with the Father, with His Son Jesus Christ, and also with the apostles and all other believers. What a wonderful thought it is that guilty sinners should ever be brought into fellowship with God the Father and with His Son Jesus Christ! And yet, that is the very truth which we have here.

Notice particularly the expression in verse three, "His Son Jesus Christ." Here we learn that Jesus and Christ are one and the same Person, and that that Person is the Son of God. Jesus is the name that was given to Him at His birth, and therefore speaks of His perfect humanity. Christ is the name that speaks of Him as God's Anointed One, the Messiah. Therefore, in the name Jesus Christ, we have a witness to His humanity and to His deity. Jesus Christ is very God of very God and very Man of very Man.

But why does John thus write concerning the subject of fellowship? The reason is that our joy may be full. John realized that the world is not capable of providing true and lasting joy for the human heart. This joy can only come through proper relationship with the Lord. When a person is in fellowship with God and with the Lord Jesus, he has a deep-seated joy that cannot be disturbed by earthly circumstances. As the poet said, "The source of all his singing is high in heaven above."

The Requirements of Fellowship (1:5–10)

Fellowship describes a situation where two or more persons share things in common. It is a communion or a partnership. John now undertakes to instruct his readers as to the requirements for fellowship with God. In doing so, he appeals to the teachings of the Lord Jesus when He was here upon earth. Although the Lord is not quoted as having used these exact words, the sum and substance of His teaching was that "God is light, and in Him is no darkness at all." By this He meant that God is absolutely holy, absolutely righteous and absolutely pure. God cannot look with favor on any form of sin. Nothing is hidden with Him, but "all things are naked and open to the eyes of Him to whom we must give account." (Hebrews 4:13).

Now it follows that in order for a person to be in fellowship with God, there can be no hiding of sin. Light and darkness cannot exist in a person's life at the same time, any more than they can exist together in the room of a home. If a man is walking in darkness, he is not in fellowship with God. A man who says he has fellowship with God and walks in darkness was never saved at all.

On the other hand, if one walks in the light, then he can have fellowship with the Lord and with his fellow Christians. As far as John is concerned in this passage, a man is either in the light or in darkness. If he is in the light, he is a member of God's family. If he is in darkness, he does not have anything in common with God because there is no darkness in God at all. Those who walk in the light, that is, those who are Christians, have fellowship with one another, and the blood of Jesus Christ cleanses them from all sin. The latter part of this verse does not mean that a Christian is constantly cleansed by the blood, but rather that the one cleansing received at conversion has continuing value. Christians are cleansed once by the blood of Christ, but washed constantly by the Word of God from defilement along the way.

Then again, fellowship with God requires that we acknowledge the truth concerning ourselves. For instance, verse eight tells us that to deny that we have a sinful nature means self-deception and untruthfulness.

In order to enter into the Christian fellowship, there must be confession of sins. "He who covers his sins will not prosper, but whoever confesses and forsakes them will have mercy" (Proverbs 28:13). The promise of God's Word is that if a man confesses his sins, God is faithful and just to forgive. He is faithful to forgive these sins, in the sense that He has promised to do so and will abide by His promise. He is just to forgive them in the sense that this forgiveness was purchased through the work of Christ, and God can righteously forgive because a perfect satisfaction has been made. In addition, God promises to cleanse the repentant sinner from all unrighteousness.

Thus, in order to enter into the Christian fellowship, a sinner must take sides with God against himself. He must acknowledge his sins and forsake them. Forgiven through the precious blood of Christ, he can now go on in happy fellowship with God. But verse 9 may also apply to the lives of those who are already saved. Just as we enter the Christian fellowship through repentance and faith, so day by day fellowship with God is maintained through confession of our sins. When we first confess our sins as penitent sinners, we received what is known as judicial forgiveness. This means that the penalty of sins has been put away once for all. As Christians, we confess our sins daily and receive parental forgiveness. This means that the happy family spirit is restored and possible parental discipline is averted. The latter is the forgiveness of a father rather than that of a judge.

Finally, in order to be in fellowship with God, we must not deny that we have committed acts of sin. God has stated over and over in His Word that all have sinned. To deny this is to make God a liar. It is a flat contradiction of His Word, and a complete denial of the reason for which the Lord Jesus came to suffer, bleed and die.

Thus we see that fellowship with God does not require lives of sinlessness, but rather requires that all our sins should be brought out into His presence, confessed and forsaken. It means that we must be absolutely honest about our condition, and that there be no hypocrisy or hiding of what we really are.

Sin Mars Fellowship (2:1, 2)

In these two verses, John gives us God's perfect standard for His people, and His gracious provision in the event of failure. The expression "my little children" might better have been translated "dear children," and refers to all the members of the family of God. God's perfect standard is then set forth in the words, "these things I write to you, that you may not sin." Because God is perfect, His standard for His people is absolute perfection. He would not be God if He said, "these things I write to you that you sin just as little as you can." God cannot condone sin in the least degree, and so He sets perfection before us as the goal. The Lord Jesus did this with the woman who was taken in the act of adultery; He said, "Neither do I condemn you; go and sin no more." (John 8:11).

At the same time, the Lord knows our frame. He remembers that we are dust, and so He has graciously made provision for us in the event of failure. This is expressed in the following words, "And if anyone sins, we have an Advocate with the Father, Jesus Christ the righteous." An advocate is one who comes to the side of another person in time of need in order to help. This is exactly what the Lord Jesus does for us when we sin. He immediately comes to us in order to restore us to fellowship with Himself. Notice that it does not say, "If any man confess his sins. . . ." As our advocate, the Lord seeks to bring us to the place where we do confess and forsake our sin.

There is something very wonderful in this verse which the student should not overlook. It says, "If any man sin, we have an advocate with the Father." It does not say with God, but rather with the Father. In other words, He is still our Father even if we sin. This reminds us of the blessed truth that though sin in a believer's life breaks fellowship, it does not break relationship. When a person is born again, he becomes a child of God. God is henceforth his Father, and nothing can ever affect that relationship. A birth is something that cannot be undone. A son may disgrace his father, but he is still a son by the fact of birth.

Notice that our advocate is Jesus Christ the righteous. It is good to have a righteous advocate. When Satan brings some accusation against a believer, the Lord Jesus can point to His finished work on Calvary's Cross and say, "Charge that sin to My account."

And the Lord Jesus is not only our advocate, but He is also the propitiation for our sins. This means that by dying for us, He freed us from the guilt of our sins and restored us to God by providing the needed satisfaction and by removing every barrier to fellowship. God can show mercy to us because Christ has satisfied the claims of justice. It is not often that an advocate (or lawyer) pays for his client's sins; yet that is what our Lord has done, and most remarkable of all, He paid for them by the sacrifice of Himself.

John adds that He is the propitiation not for our sins only, but also for the sins of the whole world. This does not, of course, mean that the whole world is saved. Rather it means that the work of the Lord Jesus is sufficient in value to save all the world, but it is only efficient to save those who actually put their trust in Him. It is because His work is sufficient for all men that the gospel can be offered to all the world. But if all men were automatically saved, there would be no need of preaching the gospel to them.

It is interesting to remember that the superscription on the Cross was written in words of Hebrew, Greek and Latin. These were the principal languages of the then-known world. It was thus proclaimed to all the world that Jesus Christ is a sufficient Savior for all men everywhere.

CHAPTER

2

Tests for Fellowship (1 John 2:3-28)

The Test of Obedience (2:3–6)

John is about to give the true marks of those who are in the Christian fellowship. The first is that of obedience. We can have assurance concerning our relationship with God if our life is characterized by a loving desire to do His will. These verses are doubtless aimed at the Gnostics who professed to have a superior knowledge of God, but who showed little interest in keeping the commandments of the Lord. John shows that such knowledge is hollow and worthless.

Notice that John describes the believer's obedience in a threefold way—keeping His commandments (verse 3); keeping His word (verse 5); walking as He walked (verse 6). There is a definite progress in the thought here. To keep His commandments is to obey the teachings of the Lord Jesus as they are found in the New Testament. To keep His word means not only obedience to what is written, but a desire to do that which we know would please Him. To walk as He walked is the full expression of God's standard for His people; it means to live as Jesus lived.

John does not imply here that the Christian life consists in faultless obedience to the will of God, but rather that the Christian habitually desires to keep His commandments and to do those things that are pleasing in His sight. John is looking at the over-all tenor of a man's life. If a man says he knows God but does not keep His commandments, then it is clear that he is not telling the truth.

On the other hand, when we keep His word, then the love of God has been perfected in us. The expression "the love of God" does not refer to our love for God, but rather to His love for us. The thought is that God's love toward us has been brought to its goal when we keep His word. It accomplishes its aim and reaches its end in producing obedience to Him.

Therefore, all who say that they abide in Him, should walk even as the Lord Jesus walked. His life, as set forth in the Gospels, is our pattern and guide. It is not a life which we can live in our own strength or energy, but is only possible in the power of the Holy Spirit. Our responsibility is to turn our lives over to Him unreservedly, and allow Him to live His life in and through us.

The Test of Love (2:7–17)

Another important mark of true believers is love for the brethren. John says that this is not a new commandment which he is writing, but an old commandment which they had from the beginning. In other words, the Lord Jesus had taught His disciples to love one another from the very beginning of His earthly ministry.

The Gnostics were always parading their teachings as being new. But the apostle urges his readers to test everything by the teaching of the Lord Jesus when He was here upon earth. There is always the danger of drifting away from that which was in the beginning. John says, "Get back to the beginning, and you will know what is true." Yet verse eight tells us that this commandment is not only an old commandment, but there is a sense in which it is also new. You see, when the Lord Jesus was here, He not only taught His disciples to love one another, but He gave them a living example of what He meant. His life was characterized by love for others. The commandment was thus true in Him when He was here upon earth. But now there is a sense in which the old commandment is new. In this dispensation, it is not only true in the Lord Jesus, but in believers also. These Christians had formerly been heathens, living in hatred and passion. Now they illustrated and embodied the great law of love in their lives.

Thus the darkness is passing whenever men receive the light of the gospel. The darkness has not all vanished because many have not come to Christ, but Christ, the True Light, is shining, and whenever sinners turn to Him they are saved, and henceforth love their fellow-believers.

In verses nine through eleven we have the contrast between love that is false and that which is true. If one professes to be a Christian and yet hates those who are truly Christians, it is a sure sign that such a one is in darkness "until now." This latter expression shows that it is not a case of backsliding that is in view. The man continues to be what he always was, namely, unsaved. On the other hand, the one who characteristically loves his brother abides in the light, and there is no occasion of stumbling in him. This may mean that the man is not in danger of stumbling himself, or that he will not cause others to stumble. Either interpretation is true. If the Christian is really living in touch with the Lord, the light illuminates his own pathway, and no one else is offended because of any discrepancy between his profession and his practice. The Gnostics had a deep hatred for those who were true to God's Word. This proved that they were in darkness, and that they walked in darkness, and that they knew not whither they went because the darkness had blinded their eyes.

As if to illustrate the brotherly love about which he has been speaking, the apostle now stops to address loving greetings to those who are members of the family of God.

First he embraces the whole family with the expression "little children" (verse 12) (more accurately "dear children"). Here there is no thought of age or spiritual development. John is speaking to all who belong to the Lord, and this is proved by the rest of the verse, "because your sins are forgiven you for His name's sake." This is true of all Christians. It is a wonderful thing to know, as a present possession, the complete remission of our sins. Notice, too, that our sins are forgiven for His name's sake. It is for Christ's sake that God forgives us our sins.

In verse thirteen, fathers are described as those who have known Christ from the beginning, mature believers who have known the sweet companionship of the Son of God and are satisfied with Him. Young men in the spiritual family are characterized by vigor and by combat. This is the period of conflict and of wrestling with the foe. Young men overcome the wicked one because they have learned the secret of victory, namely, "Not I, but Christ living in me." The little children in verse 13 are the babes in the faith. They do not know very much, perhaps, but they do know the Father. When John repeats his address to the fathers, it is the same as at the first. The reason for this is that they have achieved maturity in spiritual experience. Again the young men are addressed as those who are strong; that is, strong in the Lord and in the power of His might. They have overcome the wicked one because the Word of God abides in them. You will remember that the Lord Jesus was able to defeat Satan in the wilderness by quoting the Scriptures. This emphasizes the importance of constantly feeding on the Bible and having it ready to repel the attacks of Satan.

In verses fifteen through seventeen, we have a strong warning against the world and all its false ways. Perhaps this is addressed primarily to the young men, for whom the world often holds a special attraction, but it is a warning that applies to all the Lord's people. The world here is not the planet on which we live, or the natural creation about us. Rather, it is the system which man has built up in an effort to make himself happy without Christ. It may include the world of culture, the world of the opera, the world of art, the world of education—in short, any sphere in which the Lord Jesus is not loved and welcomed.

We are plainly warned not to love the world or the things that are in the world, for the simple reason that love for the world is not compatible with love for the Father. All that the world has to offer may be described as the lust of the flesh, the lust of the eyes and the pride of life.

- The lust of the flesh refers to such sensual bodily appetites as proceed from within our evil nature.

- The lust of the eyes applies to such evil desires as may arise from what we see.

- The pride of life is an unholy ambition for self-display and self-glory.

These three elements of worldliness are illustrated in the sin of Adam. The tree was good for food; that is the lust of the flesh. The tree was pleasant to the eyes; that is the lust of the eyes. It was a tree to be desired to make one wise; this describes the pride of life.

A. W. Pink has noted that as the devil is opposed to Christ, and the flesh is hostile to the Spirit, so the world is antagonistic to the Father. Appetite, avarice and ambition are not of the Father, but are of the world. That is, they do not proceed from the Father, but find their source in the world. Someone has defined worldliness as the love for passing things. The human heart can never find satisfaction with things.

"The world is passing away, and the lust of it." Lenski has wisely pointed out that when a bank is breaking, wise people do not deposit in it. When the foundation is tottering, intelligent builders do not proceed. So wise people do not live for a world that is passing away. "But he who does the will of God abides forever." It is the will of God that delivers us from the temptation of passing things. This, incidentally, was the life verse of D. L. Moody, the great evangelist, and these are the words which are inscribed on his tombstone, "He who does the will of God abides forever."

The Test of Doctrine (2:18–28)

We come now to another test of those who are in the Christian fellowship. That is the test of doctrine. The subject is introduced by a warning addressed to those who are babes in Christ against false teachers. Those who are young in the faith are especially susceptible to the lies of the antichrist. John's readers had been taught that an antichrist would arise prior to the coming of Christ and pretend to be Christ. Just as coming events cast their shadow before them, so prior to the rise of the antichrist, many antichrists appear. These are false teachers who offer a false Christ and a false gospel. It is remarkable that the day in which we live is characterized by the existence of many Christ-denying cults, and these all bear testimony to the fact that the coming of the Savior is near.

From verse nineteen we learn that these false teachers were professing Christians who once fellowshipped with the people of God. However, in heart they were not really one with true believers, and they showed this by going out from the fellowship. "If they had been of us, they would have continued with us." (The words "no doubt" should not be included in this verse.) Here we learn that true faith always has the quality of permanence. If a man has really been born again, he will go on for the Lord. Is not this what the Lord Jesus meant when He said, "He that endureth to the end shall be saved"? It does not mean that we are saved by enduring to the end, but rather indicates that those who do endure unto the end are really saved. The false teachers went out that they might be made manifest that they were not all of us. The Revised Version says that "they all are not of us." That is, not one of them possessed spiritual life.

But all this raises the interesting question, "How can a young believer know what is truth and what is falsehood?" The answer is given in verse twenty. We have an anointing from the Holy One and know all things. The word "anointing" refers to the Holy Spirit of God. The anointing is from the Holy One: that is, from the Lord Jesus Christ. When a person is saved, he receives the indwelling Holy Spirit, and He enables the believer to discern between truth and error. When John tells his young readers, "you know all things," he does not mean this in an absolute sense. It is not that they have perfect knowledge, but rather that they have the capacity to recognize what is true and what is not. Thus the youngest, simplest believer has the capacity of discernment in divine things that an unsaved philosopher would not have. That is why it is sometimes said that the Christian can see more on his knees than the worldling can see on his tiptoes. In the physical realm, when a baby is born, he is at once endowed with all the faculties of the human race. He has eyes, hands, feet and brains. He never gets these later. Although they enlarge and develop, there is the whole man there at first. So it is when a person is born again. He has at that moment all the faculties that he will ever have, although there will be endless possibilities for developing them.

John did not write because his readers were ignorant of the truth, but rather to confirm them in the truth that they knew, and to remind them that no lie is of the truth. The Gnostics were teaching doctrines that were contrary to the Word of God, and therefore they were lies. Their principal lie, the very basis of all their teaching, was their denial that Jesus is the Christ. As pointed out in the introduction, they taught that Jesus was a mere man and that the Christ came upon Him at His baptism. This is the great lie of some of the cults today. The Bible everywhere insists that the Jesus of the New Testament is the Jehovah of the Old Testament. It is not correct to say that the Christ came upon Jesus, but rather that Jesus is the Christ.

John is careful to point out in verse twenty-two that to deny the deity of the Lord Jesus is to deny the Father also. Some people like to believe that they worship God, but they do not want to have anything to do with the Lord Jesus Christ. The apostle says, "He is antichrist who denies the Father and the Son." In John 8:42, Jesus said that those who denied His deity neither knew the Father nor had Him as their Father. Similarly, John says in verse 23, "Whoever denies the Son does not have the Father either; he who acknowledges the Son has the Father also." Here we have the wonderful truth of the unity between the Father and the Son. You cannot have the Father unless you have the Son. This is a message which should be heeded by all Unitarians, Christian Scientists, Mohammedans, Modernists, Russellites and Jews.

The safeguard for young believers against the false teachers is given in verse twenty-four. "Let that abide in you which you heard from the beginning." This refers to the teachings of the Lord Jesus and of all His apostles. Our great safety is to stay close to the Word of God. We should test everything by "What says the Scripture?" If a teaching does not agree with the Bible, then we should reject it. If men say their teaching is in addition to the Bible, then we should reject it also. As Dr. Ironside has said, "If it's new, it's not true, and if it's true, it's not new." When we abide in the Christian doctrine, we give proof of the reality of our faith. And the promise of that faith is eternal life. When we accept the Lord Jesus, we receive His own life, namely, eternal life, and this life enables us to test all new and questionable doctrines.

John has written thus to the young believers concerning the false teachers by way of warning. He does not have any fear as to the eventual outcome when he remembers that his readers had received the anointing from the Lord Jesus. As was mentioned previously, the anointing is the Holy Spirit, and here we learn that the Holy Spirit "abides in you." This is a positive statement that once the Holy Spirit is received, He will never be taken away. Because we have received the Holy Spirit, we need not that any man teach us. This does not mean that we do not need Christian teachers in the church. God has made specific provision for such teachers in Ephesians 4:11. But this means that the Christian does not need any teaching apart from what is found in the Word of God as to the truth of God. The Gnostics professed to have additional truth, but John is saying here that there is no need for additional truth. With the Word of God in our hands and the Spirit of God in our hearts, we have all that we need for instruction in the truth of God.

In verse twenty-eight, John addresses all the dear children of the family of God, and exhorts them to abide in Him so that "when He appears, we may have confidence and not be ashamed before Him at His coming." The "we" here probably refers to the apostles, and the teaching is that if the Christians to whom John wrote did not go on faithfully for the Lord, the apostles who led them to Christ would be ashamed at the coming of Christ. This verse emphasizes the importance of follow-up work in all evangelistic endeavors. It also suggests the possibility of shame at the coming of Christ.

CHAPTER

3

More Tests for Fellowship (1 John 2:29–3:24)

The Test of Righteousness (2:29–3:10a)

The fourth family trait is righteousness. We know in the physical realm that like begets like. So it is in the spiritual. Everyone who practices righteousness is born of God. Because God is righteous, it follows that all He does is righteous, and therefore everyone born of Him is righteous. This is John's inescapable logic.

The thought of being born of God arrests John with wonder, and he calls upon his readers to take a look at the wonderful love that brought us into the family of God. We should remember that love could have saved us without making us children of God. But the manner of God's love is shown in that He brought us into His family as children. "Behold, what manner of love the Father has bestowed on us, that we should be called the *children* of God" (not sons). The Revised Version adds here "and such we are." He has put us into direct relationship with Himself.

Now as we walk about from day to day, the world does not recognize us as children of God. The people of the world do not understand us nor the way we behave. Indeed, the world did not understand the Lord Jesus when He was here upon earth. "He was in the world, and the world was made through Him, and the world did not know Him. He came to His own, and His own did not receive Him." (John 1:10–11). Since we have the same characteristics as the Lord Jesus, we cannot expect the world to understand us.

However, understood or not, we are now the children of God, and this is the guarantee of future glory. It is not yet manifest what we shall be, but we do know that when Christ appears, we shall be like Him, for we shall see Him as He is. This does not mean that we will be physically like the Lord Jesus in heaven. The Lord Jesus will have His own definite appearance, and will bear the scars of Calvary throughout eternity. Each of us, we believe, will have his own distinct features and will be recognizable as such. The Bible does not teach that everyone will look alike in heaven. However, we will be morally like the Lord Jesus Christ. We will be free from the possibility of defilement, sin, sickness, sorrow, and death.

And how will this marvelous transformation be accomplished? The answer is that one look at Christ will bring it to pass. "For we shall see him as He is." Here in life, the process of becoming like Christ is going on, as we behold Him by faith in the Word of God. But then the process will be absolutely complete when we see Him as He is: for to see Him is to be like Him. Every man who has this hope of seeing Christ and of being like Him, purifies himself even as He is pure. It has long been recognized by Christians that the hope of the imminent return of Christ has a sanctifying influence in the life of the believer. He does not want to be doing anything that he would not want to be doing when Christ returns. Notice that it says, "purifies himself, even as He (Christ) is pure." It does not say "even as He (Christ) purifies Himself." The Lord Jesus never had to purify Himself; He is pure. With us, it is a gradual process; with Him, it is a fact.

The opposite of purifying oneself is found in verse four. "Whoever commits sin also commits lawlessness, and sin is lawlessness." The translation of this verse is somewhat unfortunate. First of all, the word "commits" might better have been translated "practices" or "does." It is a matter of continual behavior, expressed by the present, continuous tense. It is possible to have sin even if there is no law. Sin was in the world between the time of Adam and Moses, but this was before God's law had been given. Thus it is not entirely accurate to say that sin is a transgression of the law, but rather that sin is lawlessness. It is insubjection to God, wanting one's own way and refusing to acknowledge the Lord as rightful Sovereign. It is in its essence placing one's own will above the will of God. Someone has said that it is opposition to a Living Person who has the right to obedience.

Now verse five tells us a Christian cannot go on practicing sin, because that would be a complete denial of the purpose for which the Lord Jesus came into the world. "He was manifested to take away our sins." To go on in sin, therefore, is to live in utter disregard of the reason for His incarnation.

Again, a Christian cannot go on in sin because that would be a denial of the One whose Name he bears. "In Him there is no sin" (verse five). This is one of the three key passages in the New Testament dealing with the sinless humanity of the Lord Jesus Christ. Peter tells us that "He *did* no sin." Paul tells us that "He *knew* no sin." Now John, the disciple who knew the Lord in an especially intimate way, adds his testimony, "In Him there *is* no sin."

"Whoever abides in Him does not sin. Whoever sins has neither seen Him nor known Him." Verse six contrasts the true believer with one who has never been born again. It can definitely be said of the true believer that he does not go on sinning. John is not here speaking about isolated acts of sin, but rather continued, habitual, characteristic behavior. This verse does not imply that when a Christian commits an act of sin, he loses his salvation. Rather, it says that when a person sins habitually, it is conclusive that he was never regenerated. The latter part of the verse proves that it is dealing with habitual practices and not individual acts. It says, "Whoever sins has neither seen Him nor known Him."

Perhaps the question arises at this point, "When does sin become habitual? How often does a person have to commit it for it to become characteristic behavior?" John does not answer these questions. Rather he puts each believer on guard, and leaves the burden of proof on the Christian himself.

Now while the Gnostics made great pretensions as to their knowledge, they were very careless about their personal lives. Therefore, John adds the words, "Little children, let no one deceive you. He who practices righteousness is righteous, just as He is righteous" (verse seven). There should be no confusion on this point: a man cannot have spiritual life and go on living in sin. On the other hand, a man can only practice righteousness through having the nature of Him who is righteous.

Some children are so like their parents that you couldn't lose them in a crowd. This is true of God's children and of the devil's children. "He who sins is of the devil, for the devil has sinned from the beginning." Here again the thought is "He that practices sin is of the devil." The devil has been sinning (continuous, characteristic behavior) from the beginning, that is, from the first time that he did sin. All his children follow him in this broad way. It should be added here, that men become children of God through the new birth, but there is no birth in connection with the children of the devil. A man becomes a child of the devil simply by imitating his behavior, but no one is begotten as a child of the devil.

In contrast, the coming of the Lord Jesus was for the purpose of destroying (or annulling) the work of the devil. The Lord could have destroyed the devil with a single word, but instead of that, He came down to this world to suffer, bleed and die that He might annul the works of the devil. If it cost the Savior so much to put away sin, what should be the attitude of those who have trusted Him as Savior?

Verse nine repeats the impossibility of one who has been begotten of God going on in sin. Some Bible students think that this verse refers to the believer's new nature, and that while the old nature can and does sin, the new nature cannot sin. However, we believe that here again the apostle is contrasting the regenerate man with the unregenerate, and is speaking of constant or habitual behavior. The believer does not have the sin habit. He does not knowingly continue in conscious sin.

The reason is that "His seed remains in him." There is considerable disagreement among Bible students as to the meaning of this latter expression also. Some think that this seed refers to the new nature, others to the Holy Spirit and still others to the Word of God. All of these are true, and therefore are possible explanations. We take it that the seed refers to the new life which is imparted to the believer at the time of conversion. Here, then, is a statement that the divine life remains in the believer. He is eternally secure. Rather than being an excuse for the Christian to go out and sin, his eternal security is a guarantee he will not go on sinning. He cannot sin habitually because he is born of God. This divine relationship precludes the possibility of continuance in sin as a practice of the life.

Here then is the fourth distinction of the children of God and the children of the devil. Those who do not practice righteousness are not of God. There is no in-between ground. There are none who are half-and-half. God's children are known by their righteous lives.

The Test of Love (3:10b–24a)

In this section we have a continuation of the second test of those who are in the family of God—the test of love. This is continued from 2:7-17. From the beginning of the Christian dispensation, it has been taught that love to one's brothers is a divine obligation. Love here is not used in the sense of friendliness or mere human affection, but it is divine love. It is loving others as Christ loved us. Actually, this cannot be done in one's own personal strength, but only as empowered by the Holy Spirit.

In verse twelve, the apostle goes back to the first recorded instance of a man who did not love his brother. Cain showed that he was of the wicked one by slaying his brother, Abel. The underlying motive for this murder is given in the words, "his works were evil and his brother's righteous." It is a basic principle in human life that wickedness hates righteousness, and this explains why the world hates the believer. The righteous life of the Christian throws the wickedness of the unbeliever into sharp relief. The latter obviously hates this exposure and instead of changing his wicked behavior, he seeks to destroy that which causes it to be so clearly seen. It would be just as unreasonable for a person to destroy a ruler or straight-edge for showing how crooked is the line that he has drawn.

"We know that we have passed from death to life, because we love the brethren" (verse fourteen). It is a remarkable fact that when a person is saved, he has an entirely different attitude toward Christians. This is one of the ways by which he receives assurance of his salvation. A man who does not love a true child of God may profess to be a Christian, but the Scripture says he abides in death. He always was dead spiritually, and that is what he still is. In the eyes of the world, hatred is not a very wicked thing, but God calls it murder. A moment's reflection will show that it is murder in embryo. The motive is there, although the act might not be committed. Thus, "whoever hates his brother is a murderer." When John says that no murderer has eternal life abiding in him, he does not mean that a murderer cannot be saved. He simply means that a man who characteristically hates his fellows is a potential murderer and is not saved.

The ultimate example of love was given to us by the Lord Jesus when He laid down His life for us. Christ is here contrasted with Cain. He gives us love in its highest expression. In one sense, love is invisible, but we can see the manifestation of love. In the Cross of Calvary we see the love that is love indeed.

John then draws a lesson from this, that we ought to lay down our lives for the brethren. This means that our lives should be a continual giving-out on behalf of other believers, and that we should be ready to die for them also if need so require. Most of us will never be required to die on behalf of others, but everyone of us can manifest brotherly love by sharing our material things with those in need. That is what is emphasized in verse seventeen. If verse sixteen suggests the most we can do for our brethren, verse seventeen suggests the least. John distinctly says that a man is not a Christian who sees a brother in need and yet withholds from him that which is necessary to satisfy that need. This does not justify indiscriminate giving to everyone, because it is possible to harm a man

The Letters of John

by William MacDonald

Exam Booklet

Student Name: ______________________________

Address: ______________________________

____

____

Course Grade:

Instructor: ______________________________

Developed as a correspondence course by
Emmaus Correspondence School,
founded in 1942.

AK-03

Printed by:
ECS Ministries
P.O. Box 1028
Dubuque, IA 52004-1028
U.S.A.

ISBN 0-940293-05-6

010203/06050403 (AK–03)

Printed in United States of America

Instructions to Students

Course Components

The course has two parts: the course textbook and this exam booklet.

The Course Textbook

The course textbook contains the lesson material that you will use in your studies.

The Exam Booklet

This includes all the exams for the course.

Exams

All the exams are in this booklet. Before taking each exam, carefully review the relevant chapter including the Bible references. When you actually come to take the exams, try to do so without reference to the chapter, your Bible or your notebook unless otherwise instructed.

Read the following instructions carefully.

1. Exams

Each exam covers one chapter (Exam 1, for example, covers Chapter 1). Do not answer the questions according to what you think or have always believed. The test questions are planned to find out if you understand the chapter material and the Scripture verses given in the chapter.

Review the exam and see how well you know the answers. If you find that you are having difficulty answering the questions, review the chapter again until you think you can answer the questions.

Record your answers in this Exam Booklet.

2. What Do You Say? Questions

For questions headed in this way, you may freely state your own opinions in answer to the questions. Your candid answers will help your instructor get to know you better as an individual. They will also help us evaluate the general effectiveness of this course.

3. How Your Papers are Graded

Your instructor will mark any incorrectly answered questions. You will be referred back to the place in the Bible or the textbook where the correct answer is to be found.

Upon finishing the course with a passing average of 70% or better, you will be awarded a credit certificate.

Group Enrollments

If you are enrolled in a class, submit your exam papers to the leader or secretary of the class who will send them for the entire group to the Correspondence School.

Returning the Exam for Grading

If you are studying this course through an Associate Instructor or associated ministry or organization, send the exams to the individual or organization from whom you obtained the course. Otherwise, send them to the address on the back cover of the Exam Booklet.

More instructions can be found at the end of the exams.

Chapter 1 Exam—The Christian Fellowship

Name ______________________________ Exam Grade ________
(print plainly)

Before starting this exam, write your name and address on the first page of this exam booklet.

In the blank space in the right-hand margin write the letter of the correct answer.

1. John's first letter is likened to

A. a company policy manual
B. a national constitution
C. a family photograph album
D. a religious creed ______

2. The Gnostics

A. claimed to have additional knowledge superior to that taught by the apostles
B. were genuine Christians but came from parts of the world outside the boundaries of the Roman Empire
C. formed a governing body in the Roman provinces and were noted for their scholarship
D. were Greek mercenaries in the pay of the Roman armed forces ______

3. Which of the following is a characteristic feature of John's letter? It contains

A. simple words and simple concepts
B. simple words but profound concepts
C. difficult words but simple concepts
D. difficult words and difficult concepts ______

4. The doctrinal foundation of all true Christian fellowship is centered in

A. Christian baptism
B. the Lord's Supper
C. the truth of the Lord's return
D. the Person of Christ ______

5. The apostles knew the reality of what they taught about Christ because they had

A. heard Him speak
B. seen and gazed upon Him
C. actually touched Him
D. experienced all the above ________

6. When He says that "God is light" John would have us understand that

A. Jesus was fair complexioned
B. God is absolutely holy
C. God dwells in the brightness beyond that of the sun
D. God is omnipotent, omniscient and omnipresent ________

7. A Christian who says that he lives in a state of sinless perfection is

A. a very holy person indeed
B. the kind of person who ought to be an elder in the church
C. self-deceived
D. someone all Christians should emulate ________

8. Those who would enjoy fellowship with God must

A. first get to heaven
B. do penance
C. attain a state of victory over every sin in his life
D. confess his sins to God and forsake them ________

9. God's standard of behavior for His people is that of

A. absolute perfection
B. relative morality
C. ritual cleanliness
D. doing our best ________

10. The Lord Jesus is presented to us by John as our

A. elder Brother
B. Advocate
C. Great High Priest
D. Prophet, Priest and King ________

WHAT DO YOU SAY? In what way is the Lord Jesus your propitiation?

____

____

____

____

Chapter 2 Exam—Tests for Fellowship

Name ________________________________ Exam Grade __________
(print plainly)

In the blank space in the right-hand margin write the letter of the correct answer.

1. Being obedient to God involves

A. keeping the commandments of the Lord Jesus
B. desiring even to do those things which would please the Lord
C. living as Jesus lived
D. all the above ________

2. An important mark of true believers is that they

A. isolate themselves in every way from the world
B. never experience temptation
C. love other true believers
D. make periodic pilgrimages to places venerated by the church ________

3. Which of the commandments is old yet new? The commandment that we

A. keep the Sabbath
B. love one another
C. give tithes to God's work
D. refrain from eating certain things which are condemned as "unclean" ________

4. The person who loves his brother in Christ is said by John to be

A. abiding in the light
B. earning his salvation
C. a true Gnostic
D. sinless ________

5. The expression "little children" in 1 John 2:12

A. refers only to the young in the faith
B. shows that John was essentially a children's evangelist
C. is intended as a rebuke to those in the Church who should have been mature Christians
D. is applied by John to all who belong to the Lord ________

6. What the world has to offer is summed up by John as

A. "vanity and vexation of spirit"
B. "the lust of the flesh, the lust of the eyes and the pride of life"
C. "avarice, appetite and ambition"
D. "the things which are seen" ________

7. Which of the following signs of the last days is specifically mentioned by John? The
   A. rebirth of the State of Israel
   B. coming of many false teachers who proclaim a false Christ and a false gospel
   C. rise of Russia
   D. discovery and unleashing of nuclear energy ________

8. The "anointing" from the Spirit primarily enables a Christian to
   A. win souls to Christ
   B. live a victorious life
   C. discern between truth and error
   D. speak in tongues ________

9. The Bible teaches emphatically that
   A. the Jehovah of the Old Testament is the Jesus of the New Testament
   B. Jehovah and Jesus are two different persons
   C. "the Christ" came upon Jesus at His baptism
   D. it is possible to deny the deity of Christ while upholding the deity of the Father ________

10. Which of the following ministries of the Holy Spirit is specifically mentioned by John in his first letter? His ministry of
   A. baptizing believers into the body of Christ
   B. permanently abiding in the heart and life of the believer
   C. convicting the lost of their sin, of righteousness and of judgment
   D. restraining the lawlessness of ungodly men ________

WHAT DO YOU SAY? Are you a truly saved person? Based on your study of this lesson how do you know?

____

____

____

____

Chapter 3 Exam—More Tests for Fellowship

Name ________________________________ Exam Grade ________
(print plainly)

In the blank space in the right-hand margin write the letter of the correct answer.

1. The true believer practices righteousness because

A. he is born of God
B. the law demands it
C. he will lose his salvation if he doesn't
D. the world expects it of him ________

2. John says that believers are called

A. "holy and true"
B. "priests of the Most High"
C. "children of God"
D. "children of eternity" ________

3. In heaven everyone will

A. have the same physical appearance as the Lord Jesus
B. look alike
C. be morally like the Lord Jesus
D. purify himself ________

4. John's definition of sin in 1 John 3:4 is that sin is

A. simply a transgression of the law
B. lawlessness and insubjection to God
C. an unfortunate tendency for which we cannot be blamed and are not really responsible
D. something we do only occasionally and in an involuntary way ________

5. Which of the following statements regarding the sinlessness of the Lord Jesus is ***NOT*** true?

A. Peter says that "He did no sin"
B. Paul declares that "He knew no sin"
C. John asserts that "in Him is no sin"
D. James says that "He became sinless" ________

6. When a person who professes to be a Christian continues to make sin the habit of his life it

A. proves he was never truly saved
B. means that he loses his salvation
C. does not really make any difference since "once saved, always saved"
D. grieves the Spirit but does not prove him to be actually an unsaved person ________

7. The phrase "His seed remains in him" is a reference to

A. the Adamic nature which all men inherit at birth
B. the old, carnal nature which continues to plague even the child of God
C. the divine life which the believer possesses
D. the resurrection of Christ from the dead ________

8. John gives a negative illustration to emphasize his teaching on love. This illustration is taken from the story of

A. Adam and Eve
B. Cain and Abel
C. David and Jonathan
D. Orpah and Ruth ________

9. John says that we can know that we have passed from death unto life because we

A. live sinless lives
B. have been baptized
C. enjoy reading the Bible
D. love the Lord's people ________

10. When John says, "If our heart does not condemn us," he is referring ***primarily*** to

A. the attitude with which we come to God in prayer
B. the attitude we adopt toward other Christians
C. the attitude we have toward questionable amusements
D. none of the above ________

WHAT DO YOU SAY? In what ways do you manifest your love for the Lord's people?

____

____

____

____

Chapter 4 Exam—Still More Tests for Fellowship

Name ______________________________ Exam Grade ________
(print plainly)

In the blank space in the right-hand margin write the letter of the correct answer.

1. John's reminder that there are other spirits abroad besides the Holy Spirit was prompted by

A. an encounter he had just had with a demon possessed man
B. the arrival at Ephesus of some false teachers
C. an outbreak of spiritism in the Church
D. his preceding reference to the Holy Spirit ________

2. The essence of the confession required of "a spirit" is

A. an acknowledgment of the historical fact that Jesus was born into the world with a human body
B. the acknowledgment that Jesus is the incarnate Christ
C. the acknowledgment that Jesus rose from the dead
D. the acknowledgment that we need to be saved by Christ ________

3. John says in 1 John 4:5 that false teachers are

A. of the world
B. of the flesh
C. of the devil
D. of all the above ________

4. Which of the following statements provides us with a key to all God's works and ways?

A. God is omnipotent
B. God is love
C. God is light and in Him is no darkness at all
D. God cannot lie ________

5. The expression "His only begotten Son" conveys the thought that the Lord Jesus is

A. God's only Son
B. God's beloved Son
C. God's unique Son
D. God's firstborn Son ________

6. The lesson enforced by the truth of God's love is that

A. all men will be saved
B. God is too kind to condemn sinners
C. God's love must be viewed apart from the redemptive work of Christ
D. since God loves us we ought to love all those in His family ________

7. According to John's letter, the invisible God is made known to the world today through

A. philosophy
B. believers in the Lord Jesus
C. religion
D. the Lord Jesus Christ ________

8. God intends believers to be

A. the terminal point of His grace
B. channels of blessing to all mankind
C. canonized by the Church
D. free from all temptation ________

9. When John says that "Whoever confesses that Jesus is the Son of God, God abides in him . . . " he is speaking of the confession

A. of sins made to a priest
B. of sins to God
C. of intellectual assent to truth
D. of a life commitment to Jesus Christ ________

10. It is pointless to say that we love God if we

A. hate our brother
B. still yield to temptation
C. are not full time missionaries
D. do not give most of our money to the Lord's work ________

WHAT DO YOU SAY? How much do you love the Lord Jesus? By what standard are you measuring your love to Him?

____

____

____

____

Chapter 5 Exam—Further Tests for Fellowship

Name ______________________________ Exam Grade ________
(print plainly)

In the blank space in the right-hand margin write the letter of the correct answer.

1. The results of faith are

A. the new birth
B. love for God and His people
C. obedience to God's commands
D. all the above ________

2. The person who overcomes the world is the person who

A. humbly believes in the Lord
B. has grasped the world's philosophies
C. becomes a renowned scientist
D. masters the principles of psychology ________

3. The reference to "He that came by water and blood" is taken in the lesson to refer to

A. the Lord's baptism and atoning death
B. the water and blood that flowed from Christ's side at Calvary
C. the Spirit of God and the blood of Christ
D. the phenomena of natural birth ________

4. Which of the following verses from 1 John 5, found in the King James Version, is omitted by many versions of the Bible?

A. Verse 4
B. Verse 5
C. Verse 7
D. Verse 8 ________

5. The emphasis of the verse omitted from many excellent translations of 1 John is on the doctrine of

A. the virgin birth
B. the Trinity
C. the resurrection of Christ
D. the second coming ________

6. One of the three "witnesses" concerning the truth is said by John to be "the water." This is a reference to

A. the Lord's baptism
B. the baptism of infants
C. the baptism of believers
D. the Word of God itself ________

7. John's statement in 1 John 5:11, 12 is really

A. a part of an ancient hymn
B. a quotation from the Psalms
C. a summary of the Christian message
D. not part of the original epistle ________

8. God will answer positively

A. all our prayers if we are saved
B. everybody's prayers whether or not they are saved
C. every prayer found in a prayer book
D. all prayers offered in accordance with His will ________

9. The textbook takes which of the following positions on the reference by John to the "sin leading to death"? It takes the position that

A. it refers to sin persisted in by a believer and unconfessed by him
B. it refers to the sin of murder
C. it refers to the sin of blasphemy against the Holy Ghost
D. it refers to the sin of apostasy ________

10. John's final word in his first letter is an exhortation against

A. idolatry
B. slothfulness
C. inconsistency
D. keeping the Sabbath ________

WHAT DO YOU SAY? Name one thing you have learnt from this chapter and how will it affect your life?

____

____

____

____

Chapter 6 Exam—John's Last Two Letters

Name ______________________________ Exam Grade __________
(print plainly)

In the blank space in the right-hand margin write the letter of the correct answer.

1. The key words in 2 and 3 John are

A. grace and peace
B. faith and hope
C. love and truth
D. joy and gladness ________

2. The text takes the position that the expression "the elect lady" refers to

A. a woman named Electa
B. the Church, the Bride of Christ
C. one of God's elect saints
D. the Jewish remnant in the Church ________

3. Paul says that false teachers make a special appeal to

A. young people
B. children
C. prominent men
D. women ________

4. Verses 5–9 of 2 John

A. give truth revealed nowhere else in the New Testament
B. summarize 1 John
C. are a prologue to the book of Revelation
D. are not included in many of the original manuscripts ________

5. Which of the following really knows God?

A. one who says that Jesus is a "god"
B. one who believes that Jesus is no more divine than any other man
C. one who says that Christ's miracles were illusions of the mortal mind
D. one who believes that God became man in the person of Jesus Christ ________

6. When a Christian knows that a person is a false teacher he should

A. refuse to allow him into his home
B. entertain him with true Christian hospitality
C. slam the door in his face as hard as possible
D. send him next door with God's blessing ________

7. The second and third letters of John

A. are identical except for a few phrases
B. present us with a study in contrasts
C. both make mention of the apostle Paul
D. were really written by two different people ______

8. Gaius was

A. apparently not too well physically
B. warned by John not to be so taken up with his physical well-being
C. rebuked by John because his spiritual health was so much poorer than his physical health
D. healed by John ______

9. Which of the following was commended by John for his hospitality?

A. Demetrius
B. Diotrophes
C. Gaius
D. Barnabas ______

10. Diotrophes is famous for his

A. ardent support of John
B. pontifical, proud and self-important spirit
C. good report of all men
D. helpfulness to itinerant evangelists ______

WHAT DOYOU SAY? Whom do you most admire? Gaius, Diotrophes or Demetrius? Why?

Returning the Exam for Grading

- After completing the exam, check it carefully.
- Make sure you have followed the directions.
- Be sure you have written your correct name and address on all material you will send to the School.
- Address the envelope correctly.
- Return only this exam booklet, not the course book.
- Put the correct postage on the envelope.
- Return all the exams at one time.

If you are studying this course through an Associate Instructor or associated ministry or organization, send the exams to the individual or organization from whom you obtained the course. Otherwise, send them to the address on the back cover.

NOTE ! !
A special page has been provided for your answers to the exams. Please submit your answers on that page.
Do not submit the exam booklet.

Set Free Correspondence Ministry
P.O. Box 940731
Plano, TX 75094

ECS Ministries
Emmaus Correspondence School
PO Box 1028
Dubuque, IA 52004-1028
United States of America

by giving him money with which to buy that which would not be good for him. However, the verse does raise very disturbing questions concerning the accumulation of wealth by Christians.

In verse eighteen we learn that our love should not be in word or tongue, but rather in deed and in truth. In other words, it should not be a matter of affectionate terms only, neither should it be an expression of what is not true. But it should be manifested in actual deeds of kindness and should be genuine instead of false. By the exercise of this real and active love to our brethren, we shall know that we are of the truth, and this will give us assurance of heart as we come before God in prayer.

"For if our heart condemns us, God is greater than our heart, and knows all things." The subject here is the attitude with which we come before God in prayer. This verse twenty may be understood in two ways. First of all, if our heart condemns us, God is greater than our heart in the sense that He is greater in compassion. While we may have intense feelings of unworthiness, yet God knows that basically we love Him and we love His people. He knows that we are His in spite of all our failures and sins.

The other view is that if our heart condemn us, God is greater than our heart in the matter of judgment. Whereas we only know our sins in a very limited way, God knows them fully and absolutely. He knows all that there is to blame in us, whereas we only know it in part. The writer leans to this latter viewpoint, although both are correct and therefore possible.

Verses twenty and twenty-two give us the attitude of one who has a clear conscience before God. It is not that this person has been living sinlessly, but rather that he has been quick to confess and forsake his sins. By doing this, he has confidence before God and boldness in prayer. Thus, "if our heart does not condemn us, we have confidence toward God. And whatever we ask we receive from Him, because we keep His commandments and do those things that are pleasing in His sight." To keep His commandments is to abide in Him. It is to live in close, vital intimacy with the Savior. When we are thus in fellowship with Him, we make His will our own will. By the Holy Spirit, He fills us with the knowledge of His will. In such a condition, we would not ask for anything outside the will of God. When we ask according to His will, we receive of Him the things for which we ask.

John further elaborates the meaning of "His commandments" in verse twenty-three. His commandment is "that we should believe on the name of His Son Jesus Christ and love one another, as He gave us commandment." This verse seems to summarize all the commandments of the New Testament. It speaks of our duty to God and to our fellow

Christians. Our first duty is to trust in the Lord Jesus Christ. Then because true faith is expressed in right conduct, we should love one another. This is the evidence of saving faith.

It should be noticed in this and other verses that John uses the personal pronouns "He" and "Him" to refer to both God the Father, and the Lord Jesus Christ without stopping to explain which is intended. He dares to do this because the Son is as truly God as the Father, and it is no presumption to speak of Them in the same breath.

The first part of verse twenty-four ends the section on love as a test of the children of God. We read, "Now he who keeps His commandments abides in Him, and He in him." To obey Him is to abide in Him, and those who abide in Him are assured of His abiding presence also.

CHAPTER

4

Still More Tests for Fellowship (1 John 3:24–4:21)

The Test of Doctrine (3:24b–4:6)

The apostle now returns to the test of doctrine. He had previously dealt with this in 2:18–28. The subject is introduced by the statement that assurance of God's abiding in us comes through the Holy Spirit. All believers have the Holy Spirit. It is He who guides them into all truth and enables them to discern error.

But having mentioned the Holy Spirit, John is reminded that there are other spirits abroad in the world today, and that the children of God need to be warned against them. Thus in verse one of chapter four he cautions the believer not to trust every spirit. The word "spirit" here probably refers primarily to teachers but not necessarily exclusively so. Just because a man speaks about the Bible and about God and about Jesus, it does not mean that he is a true child of God. We are to try, or to test or prove, the spirits, whether they be of God, because many false prophets are gone out into the world. These are men who profess to accept Christianity, but they preach another gospel altogether.

In verses two and three John gives the actual tests by which these men are to be proven. The great test of a teacher is, "What do you think of Christ?" The King James Version of the Bible says, "Every spirit that confesseth that Jesus Christ is come in the flesh is of God." Perhaps a more accurate translation would have been, "Every spirit that confesses Jesus Christ come in the flesh is of God." It is not so much the confession of the historical fact, namely that Jesus was born into the world in a human body, but rather it is the confession of a living Person, Jesus Christ come in the flesh. It is the confession that acknowledges Jesus as the Christ incarnate. And confessing Him means bowing to Him as Lord of one's life. Now if you ever hear a person presenting the Lord Jesus as the true Christ of God, you will know that he is speaking by the Spirit of God. The Spirit of God calls upon men to acknowledge Jesus Christ as Lord and to commit their lives to Him. The Holy Spirit always glorifies Jesus.

"And every spirit that does not confess that Jesus Christ has come in the flesh is not of God." This is how you can detect the false teachers. They do not confess the Jesus who was described in the previous verse. This is the spirit of antichrist which has been prophesied and which is already in the world. There are many today who are willing to say acceptable things about Jesus, but they will not confess Him as God incarnate. They will say that Christ is divine, but not that He is God. Humble believers are able to overcome these false teachers because they have the Holy Spirit within them, and this enables them to detect error and to refuse to listen to it.

The false teachers are of the world, and therefore, the source of all that they speak is the world. The world is the spring of all that they teach, and therefore the world hears them. This reminds us that the approval of the world is not a test as to the truthfulness of one's teachings. If a man simply wants to be popular, all he needs to do is to speak as the world speaks, but if he is to be faithful to God, then he must face the disapproval of the world.

In verse six, John speaks as representing the apostles. He says, "We are of God. He who knows God hears us." This means that all who are really born of God will accept the teaching of the apostles as it is found in the New Testament. On the other hand, those who are not of God refuse the testimony of the New Testament, or they seek to add to it.

The Test of Love (4:7–21)

Here John resumes the subject of love for one's brother. He emphasizes that love is a duty, consistent with the character of God. As has been mentioned previously, John is not thinking of love that is common to all men, but of that love to the children of God which has been implanted in those who have been born again. Love is of God as to its origin, and "everyone who loves is born of God and knows God. He who does not love does not know God; for God is love." Notice here that it does not say that God loves. That is true, but John is emphasizing that God is love.

Love is His nature. There is no love in the true sense but that which finds its source in Him. Someone has said that the words, "God is love," are well worth all the languages in earth or heaven. Barrett calls them, "the greatest words ever spoken in human speech, the greatest words in the whole Bible." He adds, "It is impossible to suggest even in briefest outline all that these words contain. For no human and no created intellect has ever or will ever fathom their unfathomable meaning; but we may reverently say that this one sentence concerning God contains the key to all God's works and ways—the mystery of creation, redemption and the being of God Himself."

In the verses to follow, we have a description of the manifestation of God's love. In fact, we may think of this manifestation in three tenses. In the past, God's love was manifested to us as sinners in the gift of His Son (verses 9–11). In the present, God's love is manifested to us as saints in His dwelling in us (verses 12–16). In the future, God's love will be manifested to us in giving us boldness in the day of judgment. This manifestation is to us as servants (verses 17, 18).

First of all, then, we have God's love to us as sinners. He sent His only begotten Son into the world that we might live through Him, and He sent His Son to be the propitiation for our sins. We were dead needing life, and we were guilty needing propitiation. The expression, "His only begotten Son" (verse 9), carries with it the idea of a unique relationship in which no other son could share. We might say today, "His unique Son." This makes the love of God all the more remarkable, that He would send His unique Son into the world that we might live through Him.

God's love was not shown to us because we first loved Him. We did not; in fact, we were His enemies and hated Him passionately. In other words, He did not love us because we loved Him, but He loved us in spite of our bitter antagonism. And how did He show His love? By sending His Son to be the propitiation for our sins. Propitiation means expiation, or a settling of the sin question.

Modernists today like to think of the love of God apart from the redemptive work of Christ. John here links the two as not being in the least contradictory. Denney here comments, "Note the resounding paradox of this verse, that God is at once loving and wrathful, and His love provides the propitiation which averts His wrath from us. So far from finding any kind of contrast between love and propitiation, the apostle can convey no idea of love to anyone except by pointing to the propitiation."

John now enforces the lesson of such love on us. "If God so loved us, we also ought to love one another." The "if" here does not express any doubt, but it is rather used in the sense of "since." Since God so showered His love upon those who are now His people, we also ought to love those who are members with us of His blessed family.

God's love is manifested to us at the present time in dwelling in us. The apostle says, "No one has seen God at any time. If we love one another, God abides in us, and His love has been perfected in us." In John 1:18 we read, "No one has seen God at any time. The only begotten Son, who is in the bosom of the Father, He has declared Him." In John's Gospel, we see that the invisible God is made known to the world through the Lord Jesus Christ. Here we have the expression repeated in John's Epistle, "No one has seen God at any time," but now God is manifested to the world, not through the Lord Jesus Christ, for He has gone back to heaven and is now at the right hand of God. Instead God is now manifested to the world through believers. "What a stupendous thought that now *we* should be God's answer to man's need to see Him!" (Flack). And when we love one another, His love is perfected in us. This means that God's love to us has achieved its goal. We are never intended to be terminals of God's blessings, but channels only. God's love is given to us, not that we might hoard it for ourselves, but that it might be shed abroad through us to others. When we do love one another in this way, that is proof that we are in Him, and He in us, and that we are partakers of the Holy Spirit. We should pause to marvel at the love of His dwelling in us and our dwelling in Him.

In verse fourteen, John adds the testimony of the apostolic company, "We have seen and testify that the Father has sent the Son as Savior of the world." This is a grand statement of divine love in action. "The Father has sent the Son" describes the heart-rending price He paid, and "as the Savior of the world" describes the boundless scope of Christ's work. W. E. Vine has said that, "the scope of His mission was as boundless as humanity, and only man's impenitence and unbelief put a limit to its actual effect."

Verse fifteen declares that the blessing of being indwelt by God Himself is the portion of all who confess Jesus as the Son of God. Here again it is not the confession of merely intellectual assent, but a confession that involves the commitment of one's person to the Lord Jesus Christ. No closer relationship is possible than for a person to dwell in God and to have God dwelling in him. It is hard for us to visualize such a relationship, but we might compare it, in the natural realm, to a poker in the fire, a sponge in the water, or a balloon in the air. In each case, the object is in an element and the element is in the object.

Then John adds, "And we have known and believed the love that God has for us. God is love; and he who abides in love abides in God, and he in God." The thought here is that God is love, and that love must find an object. The special object of God's love is the company of those who have been born into His family. If I am to be in fellowship with God, then I must love those whom He loves.

Verse seventeen should read, "Herein is love made perfect" (not "*our* love"). It is not our love that is made perfect at all, but God's love is made perfect with us. John is now taking us on to that future time when we will stand before the Lord. Will it be with boldness and confidence or will it be with cringing terror? The answer is that it will be with boldness, or confidence, because perfect love has settled the sin question once and for all. The reason for our confidence in that coming day is given in the words, "because as He is, so are we in this world." The Lord Jesus is now in heaven, with judgment completely behind Him. He came into the world once and suffered the punishment which our sins deserved. But He has finished the work of redemption and now will never have to take up the sin question again. As He is, so are we in this world. That is, our sins were judged at the Cross of Calvary, and we can confidently sing:

"Death and judgment are behind me,
Grace and glory lie before,
All the billows rolled o'er Jesus
There they spent their utmost power."

Just as judgment is passed for Him, so we are beyond the reach of condemnation.

Because we have come to know God's love, we have no fear of perishing. "There is no fear in love; but perfect love casts out fear." It is His perfect love that casts out our fear. I am assured of the Lord's love first of all, because He sent His Son to die for me. Secondly, I know He loves me because He indwells me at the present moment. Thirdly, I can look to the future with confidence and without fear. Truly, fear hath torment, and he that feareth is not made perfect in love. God's love has not been allowed to operate in the lives of those who fear Him. They have never come to Him in repentance and received the forgiveness of sins.

Verse nineteen reminds us that we love because He first loved us. The "him" should properly be omitted. The only reason we love at all is because He first loved us. The Ten Commandments required that man should love his God and neighbor, but the law could not produce this love. How then could God obtain this love which His righteousness required? He solved the problem by sending His Son to die for us. Such wonderful love draws out our hearts to Him in return. We say, "You have bled and died for me; I will henceforth live for You."

In verse twenty, John emphasizes the futility of professing to love God while at the same time hating one's brother. As spokes get nearer to the center of the wheel, so they get nearer to one another. Thus, as we get closer to the Lord, the more we will love our fellow-believers. Actually, we do not love the Lord a bit more than we love the humblest of His followers. John argues the impossibility of loving God whom we have not seen if we do not love our brothers whom we have seen, and closes the section by repeating the commandment which we have from God, that he who loves God should love his brother also.

CHAPTER

5

Further Tests for Fellowship (1 John 5:1–21)

The Test of Doctrine (5:1–12)

John now concludes the tests of fellowship. Here he resumes the test of doctrine, or we might also call it the test of faith. In the first three verses, we are given the results of faith. These are, first, the divine birth, then love for God, then love for one's fellow-believers, and finally obedience to God's commandments.

First of all, then, we have the divine birth. "Whoever believes that Jesus is the Christ is born of God." Belief here is not a mere intellectual assent to the fact, but rather a committal of one's life to Jesus as the Christ. If we have been truly born of God, then we will love Him. And not only so, we will love His children as well. It is good to notice here that we are to love all believers, and not just those of a certain earthly communion or fellowship.

The fourth result of faith is obedience to God's commandments. "By this we know that we love the children of God, when we love God, and keep His commandments." Those who are truly saved will be characterized by a desire to do the will of God. Our love for God is expressed in willing obedience to His commands. The Lord Jesus said, "If you love me, keep my commandments."

When John says that His commandments are not grievous, he does not mean that they are not difficult, but rather that they are the very things which born-again people love to do. When you tell a mother to take good care of her baby, you are only telling her what she loves to do. The commandments of the Lord are the things which are best for us, and the things in which our new nature takes a whole-hearted delight.

Next we learn the secret of victory over the world. The world system is a monstrous scheme of temptation, always trying to drag men away from God and from that which is eternal, and seeking to occupy him with that which is temporary and sensual. Men of the world are completely taken up with the things of time and sense. They have become the victims of passing things. Only the man who is born of God really overcomes the world, because by faith he is able to rise above the perishing things of this world and to see things in their true, eternal perspective. Thus the one who really overcomes the world is not the great scientist or philosopher or psychologist, but the simple believer who realizes that the things which are seen are temporal and that the things which are not seen are eternal. A sight of the glory of God in the face of Jesus Christ dims the glory of this world.

As we have seen, the subject of this section is faith as a test of eternal life. John has just mentioned that he that overcometh is he that believeth that Jesus is the Son of God. He now goes on to expound the truth concerning the work of the Lord Jesus Christ. He says, "This is He who came by water and blood." A great deal of disagreement has arisen over the meaning of these words. Some feel that the water and blood refer to that which flowed from the Savior's side, as recorded in John 19:34. Others feel that the water refers to the Spirit of God and that the blood refers to the blood which was shed on Calvary. Still others believe it is a reference to natural birth, where water and blood are present. We would like to suggest a fourth interpretation which takes particular account of the Gnostic heresy which the apostle is seeking to combat in this letter.

As was mentioned earlier, the Gnostics believed that Christ came upon Jesus at His baptism and left Him before His passion, namely in the Garden of Gethsemane. In other words, they would say, "The Christ did not die on the Cross, but Jesus the man died." This, of course, robs His work of any atoning value for the sins of others.

We suggest that in this verse John uses the water as an emblem of Jesus' baptism and the blood as a symbol of His atoning death. These were the two terminals of His public ministry. John is saying that Jesus was just as much the Christ when He died upon the Cross as when He was baptized in the River Jordan. This is He that came by water *and by blood,* not by water only (which the Gnostics would concede), but by water and by blood. It seems that the human heart is perpetually trying to rid itself of the doctrine of the atonement. Men would like to have the Lord Jesus as a perfect Man, the ideal Example, who has given us a marvelous code of morals. But John here insists that the Lord Jesus is not only Perfect Man, but Perfect God also, and that the Same One who was baptized in the River Jordan gave His life as a sacrifice for sinners. Men say to Christ, "Come down from the Cross and we will believe on You." If they can just eliminate the Cross from their thinking, they will be happy. But John says, "No. You cannot have the Lord Jesus Christ apart from His perfect redemptive work at Calvary."

"It is the Spirit who bears witness, because the Spirit is truth." This means that the Holy Spirit of God always bears witness to the truth concerning the Lord Jesus which John has been unfolding. He bears witness that Christ came not with water only, but with water and with blood, because this is the truth of God.

Perhaps it will surprise the student to learn that verse seven, as it is found in the King James Version of the Bible, is not actually found in the early manuscripts of the New Testament. Even such a careful scholar as John Nelson Darby omits it from his translation of the Bible as having no real manuscript authority. The student should realize that this does not at all affect the truth of the inspiration of the Scriptures. Some people think it is important to retain the verse because it mentions the three Persons of the Trinity. However, the truth of the Trinity does not depend upon this verse alone, but is found in many other portions of the sacred Scriptures.

Having stated in the previous verses the Person and work of the Lord Jesus Christ, John now goes on to state the trustworthiness of our belief in Him. He says that there are three that bear witness (the words "in earth" should not be included), the Spirit and the water and the blood: and these three agree in one. Although the Word of God should be sufficient for us, as a basis of faith, He condescends to give us a three-fold witness concerning the truth. First of all, the Spirit of God bears witness to the truth that Jesus Christ is God and that He is the only Savior of the world. The witness of the Spirit is found in the written Word of God.

Then there is the witness of the water. We believe that this refers to what happened at the baptism of the Lord Jesus. You will remember that at that time, God opened the heavens and publicly proclaimed, "This is my beloved Son, in whom I am well pleased." Thus God the Father added His own witness to God the Spirit concerning the Person of Christ.

Finally, there is the witness of the blood. On the Cross of Calvary, the Lord Jesus bore witness to Himself that He was the Son of God. No one took His life from Him; He laid it down of Himself. If He were a mere man, He could not have done this. The blood of the Lord Jesus Christ witnesses that the sin question has been settled once and for all to the satisfaction of God. All these three witnesses agree in one. That is, they are united in the testimony concerning the perfection of the Person and work of Christ.

Now John comes in with a telling argument, "If we receive the witness of men, the witness of God is greater." In everyday life, we constantly accept the word of our fellow men. If we did not, business would be at a standstill and social life would be impossible. We accept the testimony of men who may be mistaken and who may be deceivers. Now if we do this in everyday life, how much more should we trust the Word of God, who cannot fail and who cannot lie. It is most unreasonable not to believe God. His witness is absolutely credible, and when a man does accept His testimony concerning His Son, God seals the truth by giving the man the witness of the Spirit within him. On the other hand, if a man disbelieves God, he makes Him a liar; because he believes not the record that God gave of His Son. Men think that they can accept or reject God's testimony concerning Christ, but John would have them know that to reject it is to accuse God of dishonesty.

And now John summarizes the Christian message. "This is the testimony: that God has given us eternal life, and this life is in His Son." What tremendous truths these are, namely, that God has given eternal life to men, and that the source of this life is His own Son. From this, the conclusion of verse twelve is inevitable. "He who has the Son has life; he who does not have the Son of God does not have life." The teaching is unmistakable. Eternal life is not found in education or philosophy or science or good works or religion or the church. To have life, one must have the Son of God. On the other hand, if one does not have the Son of God, he does not have the life that is life indeed. Eternal life is inseparable from Jesus Christ.

Blessed Assurance (5:13–21)

We have now come to the concluding portion of the letter. First of all, John states in the clearest terms why he has written the preceding passages. The purpose is that those who have believed on the name of the Son of God may know that they have eternal life. If you have the marks of those who are children of God, then you can know that you have been born into the family of God. This verse also teaches another precious truth, namely, that assurance of salvation comes through the Word of God.

John wrote these things so that men may know that they have eternal life. In other words, the Scriptures were written that those who believe on the Lord Jesus may have assurance that they are saved. There is no need of hoping or guessing or feeling or groping in the dark. It is not presumption for one to say that he is saved. John states this in the clearest possible manner that those who have truly believed in the Lord Jesus may know that they have eternal life. (The latter part of this verse "And that you may continue to believe in the name of the Son of God" is omitted in many excellent translations of the New Testament.)

When we know that we have eternal life, needless to say, we can go before the Lord with confidence. John describes this confidence in verses 14 and 15. We know that if we ask anything according to God's will, He will hear those prayers and answer them. Indeed we should fear to pray for anything that is not in accordance with His will. Perhaps someone will say, "But how can I know the will of God?" The answer is that, in a general way, God's will is revealed to us in the sacred Scriptures, and so we should study the Word in order that we might know better what God's will is and how we can pray more intelligently.

In verse 16, the apostle gives an instance in which the believer can have confidence in prayer, but he also cites an example in which confidence is not possible. "If anyone sees his brother sinning a sin which does not lead to death, he will ask, and He will give him life for those who commit sin not leading to death." This is apparently a case where a Christian sees a fellow-believer engaging in some sinful activity. It is not sin of a nature as to bring death on the person committing it. In such an instance, the believer can ask for the recovery of the erring person, and God will give the petitioner life for them that sin not unto death.

On the other hand, there is sin unto death, and the apostle says, "I do not say that he shall pray about that." It is impossible to say with finality just what sin unto death is, and so perhaps the safest course to follow is to list various accepted interpretations and then tell which one we feel to be most correct. (1) Some feel that the sin unto death refers to sin persisted in by a believer and unconfessed by him. In 1 Corinthians 11:30, we read that some had died because they partook of the Lord's Supper without judging themselves. (2) Others feel that the sin of murder is referred to. If a Christian should, in a moment of passion, murder another person, then we should not feel at liberty to pray for his release from the death penalty, because God has already stated that it is His will that "whoso sheds man's blood, by man shall his blood be shed." (3) Still others feel that the sin referred to here is blasphemy against the Holy Ghost. The Lord Jesus said that those who attributed His miracles, which were done in the power of the Holy Spirit, to Beelzebub, the prince of demons, had committed the unpardonable sin, and that there was no forgiveness for this sin either in that age or in the age to come. (4) Others believe that the sin unto death is some special form of sin such as that committed by Moses or Aaron, Ananias and Sapphira, and which God visits with summary judgment. (5) A final explanation is that the sin of apostasy is in view, and we believe that this is the explanation which fits in best with the context. An apostate is one who has heard the great truths of the Christian faith, has become intellectually convinced that Jesus is the Christ, has even made a profession of Christianity, although he has never been truly saved. After having tasted the good things of Christianity, he completely renounces them and repudiates the Lord Jesus Christ. In Hebrews 6 we learn that this is sin unto death. Those committing this sin have no way of escape, since "they crucify again for themselves the Son of God, and put Him to an open shame." In this entire letter, John has been speaking with the Gnostics in view. These false teachers had once been in the Christian fellowship. They had professed to be believers. They had known the facts of the faith, but then they had turned their backs on the Lord Jesus and accepted a teaching which completely denied His deity and the sufficiency of His atoning work. A Christian cannot have liberty in praying for the restoration of such because God has already indicated in His Word that they have sinned unto death.

In verse 17 John says that "All unrighteousness is sin: and there is sin not leading to death." In other words, there are distinct differences in the degrees of sin, and there are sins which are not of such a serious nature as to result in death.

Beginning with verse 18, John brings his letter to a majestic close by reiterating the great certainties of the Christian faith. "We know that whoever is born of God does not sin." Of this we can be sure, that one who has the divine nature does not go on practicing sin. The reason follows. The King James Version says that "he which is begotten of God keepeth himself, and that wicked one toucheth him not." However, the Revised Version makes a very important change here. It reads, "He that was begotten of God keepeth him." A. T. Pierson considers this the most important change in the Revised Version, and comments, "The child of God is taken up into the life of Jesus Christ and that life becomes the sphere of his safekeeping." The thought is not so much that the believer keeps himself, as that He that was begotten of God (Christ) keeps him. The Inter-Varsity Commentary agrees with this view saying, "Jesus looks after His own and protects them from the assault of the devil."

The Christian answer to those who profess to have superior knowledge is this, "We know that we are of God, and the whole world lies under the sway of the wicked one." With John, there is no mincing of words. He sees only two spheres—"in Him" and "in the wicked one." All men are either saved or lost, and their position depends upon their relationship to Jesus Christ. Hear this, you Gnostics!

The third great truth is that of the incarnation. "We know that the Son of God has come." This is the theme with which John opened his Letter and with which he is now about to close it. The coming of the Lord Jesus revealed to us Him that is true, that is, the true God. God the Father can only be known through the Lord Jesus Christ. "The only begotten Son, who is in the bosom of the Father, he has declared him." (John 1:18). Then John adds, "and we are in Him who is true, in His Son Jesus Christ." Again the emphasis is that it is only as we are in Jesus Christ that we can be in God. "No man cometh unto the Father but by me." "This is the true God and eternal life." In other words, John is teaching what the Gnostics denied, namely, that Jesus Christ is God, and that eternal life is found only in Him.

And then we have John's final word of exhortation. "Little children, keep yourselves from idols." The apostle is saying in effect, "Beware of any teachings which are opposed to these realities." He wants the believers to keep themselves from any ideas concerning God, other than those which have been handed down to us by the apostles. Jesus Christ is God. Any other thought is idolatry. John is not here speaking primarily of idols carved out of wood. An idol is a substitute or a false god placed in the stead of the true. Here an idol is not so much a material thing as a false teaching.

Archbishop Alexander spoke of this appeal as "an eloquent shudder." We can think of no language that would improve on such a description, and so we would close this lesson with John's "eloquent shudder," "Little children, keep yourselves from idols. Amen."

CHAPTER

6

John's Last Two Letters (2 John; 3 John)

At first glance, it might seem that 2 John and 3 John are not of great importance, but as we examine them more closely, we realize that we would be very much poorer if we did not have them in the sacred Scriptures. Truly "all Scripture . . . is profitable." The key words of both letters are love and truth. The one shows the firmness of love, refusing to entertain those who do not teach the truth. The other shows the tenderness of love, helping those who have gone forward with the truth.

2 John

In 2 John, the apostle introduces himself as "the elder." This may refer to age or official position in the church. As to age, John was the last of the apostles who had companied with the Lord Jesus. As to official position, he surely was a bishop or overseer. Thus, we need not choose our explanation; both are correct.

The next expression "to the elect lady" is not so easy to explain. Three views are commonly held. Some believe that "the elect lady" is the church, elsewhere referred to as the bride of Christ, or a particular local church. Others think that the letter was addressed to "the Lady Electa"—her last name being Electa. Still others feel that John is writing to an unnamed Christian lady, who with all other believers is among the elect of God—chosen in Christ before the foundation of the world.

We agree with the latter view, and feel it is especially significant that this warning against anti-christian teachers should be found in a letter addressed to a woman. You will remember that sin first entered the world through Eve's being deceived by Satan. "The woman being deceived fell into the transgression" (1 Timothy 2:14). Paul speaks of false teachers who make a special appeal to women; they get into the house and capture weak women, laden with sins, led away with divers lusts, who will listen to anyone and yet are never able to come to the knowledge of the truth (2 Timothy 3:6, 7). Even today we know that the false cults visit homes during the daytime, when the head of the house is usually at work. Children need to be warned against false teachers also (verse 1). We saw this truth very clearly in 1 John 2:18–28.

John states that he loves this elect lady and her children *in the truth.* This means in the Christian faith. Those who are saved find themselves in a wonderful fellowship, loving others whom they never would have loved, were it not for their common love for the truth of God. "It is the truth of God that binds hearts together"—the hearts of all those who have known the truth.

In verse 2, the apostle writes: "Because of the truth which abides in us and will be with us forever." "Because of the truth" has two possible explanations. It may refer to the motive for loving all the saints, or it may give John's reason for writing this letter. Both are valid meanings.

"The truth which abides in us and will be with us forever." "The truth" here may refer to: (1) the Lord Jesus Christ. He said, "I am . . . the truth" (John 14:6); (2) the Holy Spirit. "The Spirit is truth" (1 John 5:6; see John 14:16, 17); or (3) the Bible. "Your Word is truth" (John 17:17). Should we not pause to marvel at our being indwelt by these three, and their being with us forever!

John's salutation is "grace, mercy and peace." Grace is undeserved favor to those who deserve the opposite. Mercy is pity shown to those who are guilty. Peace is the harmonious relationship that results from God's grace and mercy. All three of these blessings are from God the Father and from the Lord Jesus Christ. The Father is the Source and the Son is the Channel. In addition, they are *in truth and love,* and never at the expense of either of these virtues.

Now John expresses his joy at hearing that the children of the elect lady were walking in truth (verse 4). The truth is not just something to be believed with the mind, but something to be lived out in everyday behavior. Just as the Lord Jesus was the living embodiment of truth, so He expects our lives to be testimonies to the truth.

In verses 5 through 9, the apostle seems to give a short summary of the First Letter. There, you will remember, he listed the tests of life. Now in these verses, he repeats at least three of them—the test of love (verse 5), the test of obedience (verse 6) and the test of doctrine (verses 7–9).

First, he reminds his readers of the commandment to love their fellow-believers (verse 6). Love here is essentially the unselfish giving of oneself for the benefit of others. It is not "What can I get out of that person?" but "What can I do for that person?" Then, love is shown to be a walking after His commandments. We cannot truly love, in the divine sense, unless we are walking in obedience to the Lord and to the truth of God.

This brings us to the test of doctrine (verse 7). The great question is: "Did God really become Man in the Person of Jesus Christ?" The answer is a resounding "Yes." The Gnostics believed that the divine Christ came upon Jesus for a space of time. But John insists that Jesus Christ was, is and always will be God. Therefore, he warns his readers, "Look to yourselves, that we . . . receive a full reward." In other words, you stand firm in the truth concerning the Lord Jesus Christ so that our labor among you will not have been in vain, and so that you will receive your full reward.

When John says, "Whoever transgresses, and does not abide in the doctrine of Christ" (verse 9), he is speaking of false teachers. To transgress is to go beyond the allowed bounds. That is what the cults do; they claim to have new light and teach doctrines that God has not revealed in His Word. They do not stay within the bounds of the Christian revelation, or abide in the doctrine of Christ. "The doctrine of Christ" probably means the teachings which Christ brought, but it could also mean all that the Bible teaches about Christ. The apostle emphasizes in verse 9 that a cultist may claim to know God, but if he does not believe in the absolute deity and humanity of the Lord Jesus, he does not have God at all. God can only be known through His Son. "No one comes to the Father except through me" (John 14:6).

Verses 10 and 11 bring us to the heart of the letter. They give us valued advice on how to deal with false teachers who come to our doors. They do not refer to casual visitors but to anti-Christian propagandists. Should we invite them in? Give them a cup of tea? Help them financially? Buy their literature? The answer is that we should neither receive them nor bid them God's speed. These men are enemies of Christ. To show hospitality to them is to take sides with those who are against our Savior. It is possible that sometime we might let such a person into our house without knowing that he denies the Lord. These verses would not apply in such a case. But when we do know a man to be a false teacher, it would be disloyalty to Christ to befriend him.

Verses 10 and 11 do not apply to visitors generally. We often have unbelievers as guests in an effort to win them to Christ. But here it is a question of professed religious teachers who deny the deity and humanity of Jesus Christ. "Nothing should be done to give the impression that the offense against Christ is a matter of no great moment, or to put the delinquent in the way of influencing others" (C. F. Hogg). John would like to have said more to the elect lady. But he stops writing at this point in the hope of an early, personal visit, when he can speak face to face. How much more satisfactory it is to talk in personal encounter than to write with paper and ink! And how much more wonderful it will be to see the Savior face to face than to see Him by the eyes of faith, as at present! Truly then our joy will be full!

So John closes. "The children of your elect sister greet you." We do not know who they were, but we shall meet them some day and enjoy fellowship with them and with the beloved apostle John who wrote this letter, and best of all with the Savior Himself.

3 John

As we read this letter, we notice right away that it presents a decided contrast to the second letter. C. E. Tatham says, "In the Second we are commanded to keep the door of our home *closed,* whereas in the Third letter we are encouraged to keep it *open.* In the Second, we are warned against receiving deceivers; in the Third we are urged to receive and support fellow-workers in the truth. In the Second Epistle, we are put on guard against the foes of Christianity, whereas in the succeeding Epistle, we are encouraged to maintain practical fellowship with its friends."

Three men are mentioned in the letter—Gaius, Diotrephes and Demetrius. The first and third are warmly commended, whereas the second is sharply reproved.

As in the Second Letter, John speaks of himself as "the elder." He addresses the letter to the well-beloved Gaius whom he loves in the truth. Although we do not know if this is the same Gaius as is mentioned in Romans 16:23 or Acts 20:4, it is surprising how much we do learn about him in these few verses. First of all, we gather that he was a much-loved believer, a man whose whole life commended him to his fellow-Christians (verse 1). But apparently he was not too well physically, since John wishes that his bodily health might correspond to his spiritual vigor (verse 2). When John says "I pray that you may prosper," it is doubtful that he is thinking of wealth or material prosperity. Rather he is speaking of physical well-being, as suggested by the next phrase—"and be in health."

Would we want our physical condition to correspond to our spiritual? Is it not sadly true that we take better care of our bodies than of our souls? That is why F. B. Meyer wryly remarked, "It would not be desirable to express the wish of verse 2 to all our friends, because if their bodies were to correspond to the condition of their souls, they would suddenly fall into ill-health."

Verse 2 is of special interest to us also because it flatly contradicts what is taught by many so-called faith healers. They contend that all sickness is a result of sin in the life, and that if a person isn't healed, it is because of a lack of faith. This certainly wasn't true in Gaius' case, was it? His spiritual condition was good, but his physical condition was not so good. This shows that one's spiritual state cannot be argued from the bodily one.

In verse 3, the apostle speaks of the great joy he received when certain brethren testified of the truth that was in Gaius, and how he walked in it. It is good to have the truth in us but it is better to manifest the truth in our lives. We should not only hold the truth but allow the truth to hold us. Men would rather see a sermon than hear one. "There is nothing that counts for God in an age of fact like a holy life."

So important was this to John that he could say, "I have no greater joy than to hear that my children walk in truth" (verse 4). Perhaps most of us think of soul-winning as the greatest joy of the Christian life, and it is wonderful indeed to see men and women translated from the kingdom of darkness into the kingdom of the Son of His love. But who can measure the heartache to see those who professed to be saved, returning to their former life; like a sow returning to her wallowing in the mire and a dog to its vomit. On the other hand, what a thrill it is to see one's spiritual children going on for the Lord, from grace to grace. Again this emphasizes the importance of follow-up work in all our evangelistic endeavors. Gaius took a special delight in throwing open his home to those who had gone out preaching the gospel. His gracious hospitality was extended not only to those whom he knew, but to strangers as well. John says that he was faithful in this ministry (verse 5).

It does appear from the New Testament that this matter of hospitality is very important in God's sight. If we entertain the Lord's people, it is the same as if we entertained the Lord Himself (Matthew 25:40). On the other hand, failure to entertain His servants is looked upon as failure to entertain Him (Matthew 25:45). Through entertaining strangers, "Some have entertained angels unawares" (Hebrews 13:2). Many can testify that through the practice of hospitality, meals have been turned into sacraments (Luke 24:29–35), children have been converted, and families have been drawn closer to the Lord.

And then think of the rewards that are involved. Gaius' kindness was known to all the church (verse 6). But more than that, his name is forever enshrined in God's Holy Word as one who had an open home and an open heart. And even more, Gaius will yet be rewarded at the Judgment Seat of Christ, for "he who receives a prophet in the name of a prophet shall receive a prophet's reward" (Matthew 10:41). He will share in the reward of all those preachers whom he entertained. This is a good point for those who cannot preach, to remember; you can receive a preacher's reward by showing hospitality to preachers in the Name of the Lord. "God will recompense all deeds. The kindness of God shall crown the kindness of men."

Now John reminds Gaius that he will do well to bring them forward on their journey after a godly sort. "To send them forword on their journey" means "not just a friendly goodbye but adequate supplies." The expression "in a manner worthy of God," surely sets a high standard for us as we share our material things with those who preach and teach.

A special reason is given why Gaius should be helpful to these itinerant evangelists. "They went forth for His names sake, taking nothing from the Gentiles." These men looked to the Lord alone for the supply of their needs. They would not accept support from the unconverted. To do so would imply that their Master was too poor to provide for them. It might also give the unsaved a false ground of self-righteousness on which to rest. What a rebuke this is to the money-raising methods of Christendom today! And how it should remind us of the special obligation we have toward those servants of the Lord who go out in faith on the living God and who make their needs known to no one but the Lord. "We . . . ought to receive such, that we may become fellow workers for the truth." To receive them means to do everything possible to help them, for when we do, we help the truth in its onward march.

Apparently John had written along this line to the church, but his letter was intercepted by a man named Diotrephes, who had an exaggerated view of his own importance. He was a virtual dictator in the assembly, a little pope away from Rome. "Pride of place is his sin, an inflated sense of his own importance and a violent jealousy for what he regarded as his own prerogative, which no doubt he identified with the autonomy of the local church." Diotrephes had forgotten that Christ is the Head of the church—if he ever knew it. He had forgotten that the Holy Spirit was the Vicar or Representative of Christ in the church. No mere man has the right to take charge, to make decisions, to receive or to refuse. Such conduct is tyranny, and God hates it. Doubtless Diotrephes excused his behavior on the ground that he was contending for the truth. But that was, of course, a lie! He was doing untold harm to the truth by refusing those who preached it. Think of him—refusing the apostle John on the pretext of being faithful to God. And not only John, but other brethren as well.

Not only did he refuse these true believers, but he excommunicated those who did receive them. He was a power-mad creature, prating against God's true servants with malicious words. John will remember him on his next visit to that assembly. Such self-styled dictators cannot stand being openly denounced from the Word of God. Their continuance in power depends on secret meetings and upon a reign of fear and intimidation.

Gaius is exhorted to turn away from such evil behavior and to follow that which is good (verse 11). Good works are an evidence of relationship with God. That being so, the apostle seems to cast grave doubt on the spiritual state of Diotrephes.

Demetrius is introduced at this point (verse 12). Perhaps he was the bearer of this letter. At any rate, he had good report of all men and of the truth itself. F. B. Hole says, "Note, it is not that he bore witness to the truth, but that the truth bore witness to him. Demetrius was not the standard by which truth was tested. The truth was the standard by which he was tested; and having been so tested, he stood approved."

Now John closes in much the same way as he closed the Second Letter—delaying further discussion until face to face reunion (verse 13). We are indebted to him for these letters, giving us an insight into life in the early days of Christianity, and setting forth timeless instruction for the people of God. Soon we shall speak face to face in heaven, and then we shall understand more fully the occasional obscurities of divine revelation.